48301440R00054

MW01205596

Made in United States
Orlando, FL
26 June 2024

I Hope You're Loving Your Notebook

Can I ask you to take 60 seconds to review it?

Your review is the most helpful feedback for me as the author, and for others just like you looking for Hebrew resources.

Toda Rabah - thank you so much!

WHERE TO SUBMIT YOUR REVIEW?

Scan this, OR:

If you ordered the notebook: On your Amazon orders tap the notebook › Scroll to 'How's your item?" › Tap "Write a review".

If you ordered OR were gifted the notebook: Search "Hebrew by Inbal" on Amazon › tap on the Notebook › scroll to "Customer Review" › tap "Write a Review".

FINAL FORM

THESE LETTERS CHANGE IN SHAPE (ONLY) WHEN APPEARING AT THE END OF A WORD:

KHAF SOFIT	/KHAF SO-FEET/	כף סופית	ך ך ך	11
MEM SOFIT	/MEM SO-FEET/	מם סופית	ם ם ם	13
NUN SOFIT	/NOON SO-FEET/	נון סופית	ן ן	14
FE SOFIT	/FE SO-FEET/	פא סופית	ף ף ף	17
TSADI SOFIT	/TSA-DEE SO-FEET/	צדי סופית	ץ ץ ץ	18

NO DUGESH /DA-GESH/

THESE LETTERS CHANGE IN SOUND WHEN THEIR DOT (DUGESH) IS REMOVED:*

VET	/VET/	בית	ב ב ב	2
KHAF	/KHAF/	כף	ך כ כ	11
FE	/FE/	פא	ף פ פ	17

* 3 ADDITIONAL LETTERS IN THIS CATEGORY ARE GIMEL, DALET, TAV. THEY ARE NOT MENTIONED WITH THE OTHERS BECAUSE THERE IS NO NOTICEABLE CHANGE IN THEIR SOUND WHEN THEIR DOT (DUGESH) IS REMOVED.

TAKE YOUR HEBREW LEARNING TO THE NEXT LEVEL WITH MY COMPREHENSIVE ONLINE RESOURCES:

Scan the QR code below or go to

HEBREWBYINBAL.COM

to maximize the benefits of your notebook, advance your Hebrew with my guides, lessons, and programs, and to ask your Hebrew teacher (me!) anything.

Click the Notebook on my website to watch videos sounding & writing the letters, explaining the PSP (Phonetic System for Pronunciation), and more.

Download my free guide;
Follow me on YouTube & on Instagram for free daily bite size lessons;
Get lessons to your inbox, and more - all at HEBREWBYINBAL.COM

@hebrewbyinbal

YOUR ALPHABET SHEET

In the next pages you will find a complete list of Hebrew letters. Each letter is detailed as follows:

The letter name in Hebrew

Print traditional / Biblical letter writing

Letter no. in the Alphabet

PSP* pronunciation of the letter name

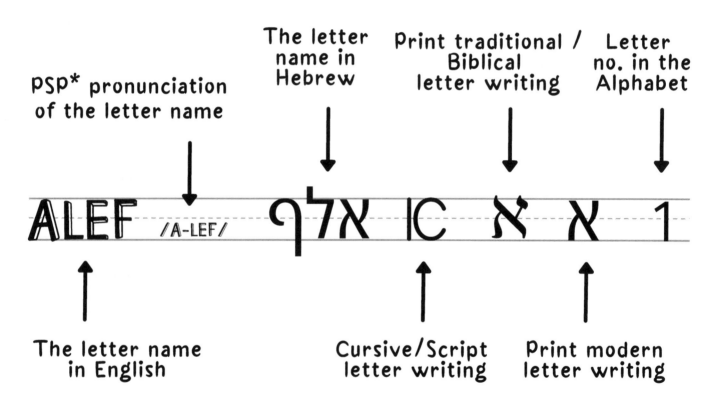

ALEF /A-LEF/ אלף IC א א 1

The letter name in English

Cursive/Script letter writing

Print modern letter writing

* Watch my videos sounding & writing the letters, how to use the PSP (Phonetic System for Pronunciation) and more!

WRITE AND READ FROM RIGHT TO LEFT

WRITE AND READ FROM RIGHT TO LEFT

WRITE AND READ FROM RIGHT TO LEFT

WRITE AND READ FROM RIGHT TO LEFT

WRITE AND READ FROM RIGHT TO LEFT

WRITE AND READ FROM RIGHT TO LEFT

WRITE AND READ FROM RIGHT TO LEFT

WRITE AND READ FROM RIGHT TO LEFT

WRITE AND READ FROM RIGHT TO LEFT

WRITE AND READ FROM RIGHT TO LEFT

WRITE AND READ FROM RIGHT TO LEFT

WRITE AND READ FROM RIGHT TO LEFT

WRITE AND READ FROM RIGHT TO LEFT

WRITE AND READ FROM RIGHT TO LEFT

WRITE AND READ FROM RIGHT TO LEFT

WRITE AND READ FROM RIGHT TO LEFT

WRITE AND READ FROM RIGHT TO LEFT

WRITE AND READ FROM RIGHT TO LEFT

WRITE AND READ FROM RIGHT TO LEFT

WRITE AND READ FROM RIGHT TO LEFT

WRITE AND READ FROM RIGHT TO LEFT

WRITE AND READ FROM RIGHT TO LEFT

WRITE AND READ FROM RIGHT TO LEFT

WRITE AND READ FROM RIGHT TO LEFT

WRITE AND READ FROM RIGHT TO LEFT

WRITE AND READ FROM RIGHT TO LEFT

WRITE AND READ FROM RIGHT TO LEFT

WRITE AND READ FROM RIGHT TO LEFT

WRITE AND READ FROM RIGHT TO LEFT

WRITE AND READ FROM RIGHT TO LEFT

WRITE AND READ FROM RIGHT TO LEFT

WRITE AND READ FROM RIGHT TO LEFT

WRITE AND READ FROM RIGHT TO LEFT

WRITE AND READ FROM RIGHT TO LEFT

WRITE AND READ FROM RIGHT TO LEFT

WRITE AND READ FROM RIGHT TO LEFT

WRITE AND READ FROM RIGHT TO LEFT

WRITE AND READ FROM RIGHT TO LEFT

WRITE AND READ FROM RIGHT TO LEFT

WRITE AND READ FROM RIGHT TO LEFT

WRITE AND READ FROM RIGHT TO LEFT

WRITE AND READ FROM RIGHT TO LEFT

WRITE AND READ FROM RIGHT TO LEFT

WRITE AND READ FROM RIGHT TO LEFT

WRITE AND READ FROM RIGHT TO LEFT

WRITE AND READ FROM RIGHT TO LEFT

WRITE AND READ FROM RIGHT TO LEFT

WRITE AND READ FROM RIGHT TO LEFT

WRITE AND READ FROM RIGHT TO LEFT

WRITE AND READ FROM RIGHT TO LEFT

WRITE AND READ FROM RIGHT TO LEFT

WRITE AND READ FROM RIGHT TO LEFT

WRITE AND READ FROM RIGHT TO LEFT

WRITE AND READ FROM RIGHT TO LEFT

WRITE AND READ FROM RIGHT TO LEFT

WRITE AND READ FROM RIGHT TO LEFT

WRITE AND READ FROM RIGHT TO LEFT

WRITE AND READ FROM RIGHT TO LEFT

WRITE AND READ FROM RIGHT TO LEFT

WRITE AND READ FROM RIGHT TO LEFT

WRITE AND READ FROM RIGHT TO LEFT

WRITE AND READ FROM RIGHT TO LEFT

WRITE AND READ FROM RIGHT TO LEFT

WRITE AND READ FROM RIGHT TO LEFT

WRITE AND READ FROM RIGHT TO LEFT

WRITE AND READ FROM RIGHT TO LEFT

WRITE AND READ FROM RIGHT TO LEFT

WRITE AND READ FROM RIGHT TO LEFT

WRITE AND READ FROM RIGHT TO LEFT

WRITE AND READ FROM RIGHT TO LEFT

WRITE AND READ FROM RIGHT TO LEFT

WRITE AND READ FROM RIGHT TO LEFT

WRITE AND READ FROM RIGHT TO LEFT

WRITE AND READ FROM RIGHT TO LEFT

WRITE AND READ FROM RIGHT TO LEFT

WRITE AND READ FROM RIGHT TO LEFT

WRITE AND READ FROM RIGHT TO LEFT

WRITE AND READ FROM RIGHT TO LEFT

WRITE AND READ FROM RIGHT TO LEFT

WRITE AND READ FROM RIGHT TO LEFT

WRITE AND READ FROM RIGHT TO LEFT

WRITE AND READ FROM RIGHT TO LEFT

WRITE AND READ FROM RIGHT TO LEFT

WRITE AND READ FROM RIGHT TO LEFT

WRITE AND READ FROM RIGHT TO LEFT

WRITE AND READ FROM RIGHT TO LEFT

WRITE AND READ FROM RIGHT TO LEFT

WRITE AND READ FROM RIGHT TO LEFT

WRITE AND READ FROM RIGHT TO LEFT

WRITE AND READ FROM RIGHT TO LEFT